THE JPS B'NAI MITZVAH TORAH COMMENTARY

Ḥayyei Sarah (Genesis 23:1–25:18)
Haftarah (1 Kings 1:1–31)

Rabbi Jeffrey K. Salkin

The Jewish Publication Society · Philadelphia
University of Nebraska Press · Lincoln

INTRODUCTION

News flash: the most important thing about becoming bar or bat mitzvah isn't the party. Nor is it the presents. Nor even being able to celebrate with your family and friends—as wonderful as those things are. Nor is it even standing before the congregation and reading the prayers of the liturgy—as important as that is.

No, the most important thing about becoming bar or bat mitzvah is sharing Torah with the congregation. And why is that? Because of all Jewish skills, that is the most important one.

Here is what is true about rites of passage: you can tell what a culture values by the tasks it asks its young people to perform on their way to maturity. In American culture, you become responsible for driving, responsible for voting, and yes, responsible for drinking responsibly.

In some cultures, the rite of passage toward maturity includes some kind of trial, or a test of strength. Sometimes, it is a kind of "outward bound" camping adventure. Among the Maasai tribe in Africa, it is traditional for a young person to hunt and kill a lion. In some Hispanic cultures, fifteen year-old girls celebrate the *quinceañera*, which marks their entrance into maturity.

What is Judaism's way of marking maturity? It combines both of these rites of passage: *responsibility* and *test*. You show that you are on your way to becoming a *responsible* Jewish adult through a public *test* of strength and knowledge—reading or chanting Torah, and then teaching it to the congregation.

This is the most important Jewish ritual mitzvah (commandment), and that is how you demonstrate that you are, truly, bar or bat mitzvah—old enough to be responsible for the mitzvot.

What Is Torah?

So, what exactly is the Torah? You probably know this already, but let's review.

The Torah (teaching) consists of "the five books of Moses," sometimes also called the *chumash* (from the Hebrew word *chameish,* which means "five"), or, sometimes, the Greek word Pentateuch (which means "the five teachings").

Here are the five books of the Torah, with their common names and their Hebrew names.

> **Genesis (The beginning), which in Hebrew is Bere'shit (from the first words—"When God began to create").** Bere'shit spans the years from Creation to Joseph's death in Egypt. Many of the Bible's best stories are in Genesis: the creation story itself; Adam and Eve in the Garden of Eden; Cain and Abel; Noah and the Flood; and the tales of the Patriarchs and Matriarchs, Abraham, Isaac, Jacob, Sarah, Rebekah, Rachel, and Leah. It also includes one of the greatest pieces of world literature, the story of Joseph, which is actually the oldest complete novel in history, comprising more than one-quarter of all Genesis.

> **Exodus (Getting out), which in Hebrew is Shemot (These are the names).** Exodus begins with the story of the Israelite slavery in Egypt. It then moves to the rise of Moses as a leader, and the Israelites' liberation from slavery. After the Israelites leave Egypt, they experience the miracle of the parting of the Sea of Reeds (or "Red Sea"); the giving of the Ten Commandments at Mount Sinai; the idolatry of the Golden Calf; and the design and construction of the Tabernacle and of the ark for the original tablets of the law, which our ancestors carried with them in the desert. Exodus also includes various ethical and civil laws, such as "You shall not wrong a stranger or oppress him, for you were strangers in the land of Egypt" (22:20).

> **Leviticus (about the Levites), or, in Hebrew, Va-yikra' (And God called).** It goes into great detail about the kinds of sacrifices that the ancient Israelites brought as offerings; the laws of ritual purity; the animals that were permitted and forbidden for eating (the beginnings of the tradition of kashrut, the Jewish dietary laws); the diagnosis of various skin diseases; the ethical laws of holiness; the ritual calendar of the Jewish year; and various agricultural laws concerning the treatment of the Land of Israel. Leviticus is basically the manual of ancient Judaism.

> Numbers (because the book begins with the census of the Israelites), or, in Hebrew, Be-midbar (In the wilderness). The book describes the forty years of wandering in the wilderness and the various rebellions against Moses. The constant theme: "Egypt wasn't so bad. Maybe we should go back." The greatest rebellion against Moses was the negative reports of the spies about the Land of Israel, which discouraged the Israelites from wanting to move forward into the land. For that reason, the "wilderness generation" must die off before a new generation can come into maturity and finish the journey.

> Deuteronomy (The repetition of the laws of the Torah), or, in Hebrew, Devarim (The words). The final book of the Torah is, essentially, Moses's farewell address to the Israelites as they prepare to enter the Land of Israel. Here we find various laws that had been previously taught, though sometimes with different wording. Much of Deuteronomy contains laws that will be important to the Israelites as they enter the Land of Israel—laws concerning the establishment of a monarchy and the ethics of warfare. Perhaps the most famous passage from Deuteronomy contains the *Shema*, the declaration of God's unity and uniqueness, and the *Ve-ahavta*, which follows it. Deuteronomy ends with the death of Moses on Mount Nebo as he looks across the Jordan Valley into the land that he will not enter.

Jews read the Torah in sequence—starting with Bere'shit right after Simchat Torah in the autumn, and then finishing Devarim on the following Simchat Torah. Each Torah portion is called a parashah (division; sometimes called a *sidrah*, a place in the order of the Torah reading). The stories go around in a full circle, reminding us that we can always gain more insights and more wisdom from the Torah. This means that if you don't "get" the meaning this year, don't worry—it will come around again.

And What Else? The Haftarah

We read or chant the Torah from the Torah scroll—the most sacred thing that a Jewish community has in its possession. The Torah is written without vowels, and the ability to read it and chant it is part of the challenge and the test.

But there is more to the synagogue reading. Every Torah reading has an accompanying haftarah reading. Haftarah means "conclusion," because there was once a time when the service actually ended with that reading. Some scholars believe that the reading of the haftarah originated at a time when non-Jewish authorities outlawed the reading of the Torah, and the Jews read the haftarah sections instead. In fact, in some synagogues, young people who become bar or bat mitzvah read very little Torah and instead read the entire haftarah portion.

The haftarah portion comes from the Nevi'im, the prophetic books, which are the second part of the Jewish Bible. It is either read or chanted from a Hebrew Bible, or maybe from a booklet or a photocopy.

The ancient sages chose the haftarah passages because their themes reminded them of the words or stories in the Torah text. Sometimes, they chose *haftarah* with special themes in honor of a festival or an upcoming festival.

Not all books in the prophetic section of the Hebrew Bible consist of prophecy. Several are historical. For example:

The book of Joshua tells the story of the conquest and settlement of Israel.

The book of Judges speaks of the period of early tribal rulers who would rise to power, usually for the purpose of uniting the tribes in war against their enemies. Some of these leaders are famous: Deborah, the great prophetess and military leader, and Samson, the biblical strong man.

The books of Samuel start with Samuel, the last judge, and then move to the creation of the Israelite monarchy under Saul and David (approximately 1000 BCE).

The books of Kings tell of the death of King David, the rise of King Solomon, and how the Israelite kingdom split into the Northern Kingdom of Israel and the Southern Kingdom of Judah (approximately 900 BCE).

And then there are the books of the prophets, those spokesmen for God whose words fired the Jewish conscience. Their names are immortal: Isaiah, Jeremiah, Ezekiel, Amos, Hosea, among others.

Someone once said: "There is no evidence of a biblical prophet ever being invited back a second time for dinner." Why? Because the prophets were tough. They had no patience for injustice, apathy, or hypocrisy. No one escaped their criticisms. Here's what they taught:

> God commands the Jews to behave decently toward one another. In fact, God cares more about basic ethics and decency than about ritual behavior.
> God chose the Jews *not* for special privileges, but for special duties to humanity.
> As bad as the Jews sometimes were, there was always the possibility that they would improve their behavior.
> As bad as things might be now, it will not always be that way. Someday, there will be universal justice and peace. Human history is moving forward toward an ultimate conclusion that some call the Messianic Age: a time of universal peace and prosperity for the Jewish people and for all the people of the world.

Your Mission—To Teach Torah to the Congregation

On the day when you become bar or bat mitzvah, you will be reading, or chanting, Torah—in Hebrew. You will be reading, or chanting, the haftarah—in Hebrew. That is the major skill that publicly marks the becoming of bar or bat mitzvah. But, perhaps even more important than that, you need to be able to teach something about the Torah portion, and perhaps the haftarah as well.

And that is where this book comes in. It will be a very valuable resource for you, and your family, in the b'nai mitzvah process.

Here is what you will find in it:

> A brief **summary** of every Torah portion. This is a basic overview of the portion; and, while it might not refer to everything in the Torah portion, it will explain its most important aspects.
> A list of the **major ideas** in the Torah portion. The purpose: to make the Torah portion real, in ways that we can relate to. Every Torah portion contains unique ideas, and when you put all

of those ideas together, you actually come up with a list of Judaism's most important ideas.

> Two **divrei Torah** ("words of Torah," or "sermonettes") for each portion. These *divrei Torah* explain significant aspects of the Torah portion in accessible, reader-friendly language. Each *devar Torah* contains references to **traditional** Jewish sources (those that were written before the modern era), as well as **modern** sources and quotes. We have searched, far and wide, to find sources that are unusual, interesting, and not just the "same old stuff" that many people already know about the Torah portion. Why did we include these minisermons in the volume? Not because we want you to simply copy those sermons and pass them off as your own (that would be cheating), though you are free to quote from them. We included them so that you can see what is possible—how you can try to make meaning for yourself out of the words of Torah.

> **Connections:** This is perhaps the most valuable part. It's a list of questions that you can ask yourself, or that others might help you think about—any of which can lead to the creation of your *devar Torah*.

Note: you don't have to like everything that's in a particular Torah portion. Some aren't that loveable. Some are hard to understand; some are about religious practices that people today might find confusing, and even offensive; some contain ideas that we might find totally outmoded.

But this doesn't have to get in the way. After all, most kids spend a lot of time thinking about stories that contain ideas that modern people would find totally bizarre. Any good medieval fantasy story falls into that category.

And we also believe that, if you spend just a little bit of time with those texts, you can begin to understand what the author was trying to say.

This volume goes one step further. Sometimes, the haftarah comes off as a second thought, and no one really thinks about it. We have tried to solve that problem by including a **summary** of each haftarah, and then a mini-sermon on the haftarah. This will help you learn how these sacred words are relevant to today's world, and even to your own life.

All Bible quotations come from the NJPS translation, which is found in the many different editions of the JPS TANAKH; in the Conservative movement's *Etz Hayim: Torah and Commentary;* in the Reform movement's *Torah: A Modern Commentary;* and in other Bible commentaries and study guides.

How Do I Write a *Devar Torah?*

It really is easier than it looks.

There are many ways of thinking about the *devar Torah.* It is, of course, a short sermon on the meaning of the Torah (and, perhaps, the haftarah) portion. It might even be helpful to think of the *devar Torah* as a "book report" on the portion itself.

The most important thing you can know about this sacred task is: *Learn* the words. *Love* the words. Teach people what it could mean to *live* the words.

Here's a basic outline for a *devar Torah:*

"My Torah portion is (name of portion)_____ ,
   from the book of _____ , chapter

_____ .

"In my Torah portion, we learn that_____
   (Summary of portion)
"For me, the most important lesson of this Torah portion is (what
   is the best thing in the portion? Take the portion as a whole;
   your *devar Torah* does not have to be only, or specifically, on the
   verses that you are reading).
"As I learned my Torah portion, I found myself wondering:
   ➤ *Raise a question that the Torah portion itself raises.*
   ➤ *"Pick a fight"* with the portion. Argue with it.
   ➤ *Answer a question* that is listed in the "Connections" section of
     each Torah portion.
   ➤ *Suggest a question to your rabbi* that you would want the rabbi
     to answer in his or her own *devar Torah* or sermon.

"I have lived the values of the Torah by _____
  (here, you can talk about how the Torah portion relates to your
  own life. If you have done a mitzvah project, you can talk about
  that here).

How To Keep It from Being Boring
(and You from Being Bored)

Some people just don't like giving traditional speeches. From our per-
spective, that's really okay. Perhaps you can teach Torah in a different
way—one that makes sense to you.

> Write an "open letter" to one of the characters in your Torah por-
  tion. "Dear Abraham: I hope that your trip to Canaan was not too
  hard . . ." "Dear Moses: Were you afraid when you got the Ten
  Commandments on Mount Sinai? I sure would have been . . ."

> Write a news story about what happens. Imagine yourself to
  be a television or news reporter. "Residents of neighboring cities were horrified yesterday as the wicked cities of Sodom and
  Gomorrah were burned to the ground. Some say that God was
  responsible . . ."

> Write an imaginary interview with a character in your Torah portion.

> Tell the story from the point of view of another character, or a mi-
  nor character, in the story. For instance, tell the story of the Gar-
  den of Eden from the point of view of the serpent. Or the story
  of the Binding of Isaac from the point of view of the ram, which
  was substituted for Isaac as a sacrifice. Or perhaps the story of
  the sale of Joseph from the point of view of his coat, which was
  stripped off him and dipped in a goat's blood.

> Write a poem about your Torah portion.

> Write a song about your Torah portion.

> Write a play about your Torah portion, and have some friends act
  it out with you.

> Create a piece of artwork about your Torah portion.

The bottom line is: Make this a joyful experience. Yes—it could
even be fun.

The Very Last Thing You Need to Know at This Point

The Torah scroll is written without vowels. Why? Don't *sofrim* (Torah scribes) know the vowels?

Of course they do.

So, why do they leave the vowels out?

One reason is that the Torah came into existence at a time when sages were still arguing about the proper vowels, and the proper pronunciation.

But here is another reason: The Torah text, as we have it today, and as it sits in the scroll, is actually *an unfinished work*. Think of it: the words are just sitting there. Because they have no vowels, it is as if they have no voice.

When we read the Torah publicly, we give voice to the ancient words. And when we find meaning in those ancient words, and we talk about those meanings, those words jump to life. They enter our lives. They make our world deeper and better.

Mazal tov to you, and your family. This is your journey toward Jewish maturity. Love it.

THE TORAH

❖ Ḥayyei Sarah: Genesis 23:1–25:18

Abraham's wife Sarah dies—maybe from a broken heart, thinking that
Isaac is dead (remember how Abraham almost offered him up as a sacrifice?). Abraham—devoted husband that he is—buys a burial place
for Sarah, outside the future city of Hebron.

With the death of Sarah, Abraham realizes that he's not going to
be around forever. He knows that Isaac needs a wife, and so he sends
his servant back to Aram-naharaim to find one for him. The servant
returns home with Rebekah.

Abraham marries again and has more children. These children drift
out of the Jewish story—at least for a while. When Abraham finally
dies, his sons Isaac and Ishmael bury him in the cave of Machpelah
with Sarah. They don't have anything to say to each other, but at least
they are together again. Sometimes, rifts in families can heal.

Summary

› Sarah dies and Abraham is determined to find a proper burial place for her. Abraham pays full price for the burial site. That site—the cave of Machpelah—became the burial place for all the Patriarchs and Matriarchs, with the exception of Rachel, Jacob's wife. (23:1–20)

› Abraham wants to keep Isaac close to home, and he doesn't want him to marry a Canaanite woman. And so, his servant goes and finds a wife for him from among Abraham's relatives. (24:1–61)

› Rebekah and Isaac meet, and it is love at first sight. (24:62–66)

› Abraham takes another wife, and (believe it or not!) has more children. (25:1–6)

› Abraham dies, and his sons, Isaac and Ishmael, reunite to bury him. (25:7–11)

The Big Ideas

› **Honoring the dead (*k'vod ha-met*) is central to the Jewish way of life.** The way that we treat the dead is one of the greatest tests of our humanity. For this reason, the purchase of land for a cemetery is generally one of the first things a new Jewish community will do.

› **The Land of Israel is precious to Jews.** In the Torah portion, Abraham purchases a burial place for Sarah, which will wind up being the burial site for all the Patriarchs and Matriarchs (except Rachel). He paid a lot for that piece of land—far more than it was actually worth. The Land of Israel is so precious to Jews that they have been willing to sacrifice almost anything for it—not only money (early Zionist settlers purchased swampland in Israel for exorbitant rates in the 1800s), but life as well.

› **Marrying within the Jewish people is an important Jewish value.** That is why Abraham took great pains to send his servant back to their "home country"—in order to find a member of the extended family for Isaac to marry. Abraham did not want Isaac to marry a Canaanite. This preference for in-marriage has been a Jewish tradition for thousands of years. That is how Jews kept the Jewish people together, and passed values and traditions from one generation to the next. Today, many Jews marry non-Jews; fortunately, many of the children of those marriages are raised as Jews.

› **Kindness to animals is an important mitzvah.** The story of Rebekah at the well underscores this value. Abraham's servant knew that the woman for Isaac would be the one who offered to feed and water his camels. You can learn a lot about someone by watching how he or she treats animals. For that reason, having pets is a great way to develop responsibility and character.

› **Families can always heal themselves.** We learn this from the brief passage in which Isaac and Ishmael meet once again to bury their father, Abraham. The brothers had been separated from each other for many years. Often, family celebrations and shared sadness bring people together.

Divrei Torah

THIS LAND IS OUR LAND

This Torah portion is filled with famous "firsts." Sarah is the first Jew to die, and Abraham is the first person in the Torah to cry (at Sarah's death). Later on in the Torah portion, Isaac becomes the first person in the Bible to love a spouse (Rebekah).

There is one more famous "first." When Abraham purchases the cave of Machpelah as a burial place, he becomes the first Jew to purchase property in the Land of Israel.

But wait: hadn't God already promised the Land of Israel to Abraham and his descendants?

Yes, but God's promise wasn't enough. After all, who would believe him—"This land is mine, because God said so"? Abraham needed to stake his own claim to the Land of Israel. He needed to buy his own piece of it. And more than this: the purchase of Machpelah was not going to be a behind-the-scenes, private sale of land. No, it was going to be out in the open, in the sight of all who were gathered there. They needed to see the sale; they needed to hear the sale; they had to be witnesses.

And why? Because Abraham could already predict what people would say in the future—that the Jews had no claim to the Land of Israel. (In fact, they are still saying precisely that.) A midrash says, "Machpelah is one of the places in the Land of Israel that no one can say was stolen."

Abraham not only bought the piece of land for all to see. He also overpaid for it! Scholars have said that with the amount of money that Abraham spent for the cave he could have purchased an entire village. That pattern of overpaying has also continued. In the 1880s, when Jews started to purchase property in the Land of Israel, it was mostly swampland—and yet, they gladly paid generously for it.

It's not enough for God to promise the Land of Israel to the Jewish people. Abraham needed to make that divine promise into a reality. Jews are still making that promise into a reality, and that is how they have built their people and their connection to the land. In the words of an old Zionist folk song: "We have come to the land, to build and to be rebuilt within it."

In this way, the Land of Israel is like the Torah. Yes, God gave the Torah, but we need to interpret it. God promised the Land of Israel, but we need to build it. That is part of what it means for Jews to be partners with God.

WHY KINDNESS TO ANIMALS MATTERS

We can imagine Abraham's servant (usually assumed to be Eliezer, based on Gen. 15:2), saying to himself: "I cannot believe that I agreed to do this. Yes, I love my master. I would do almost anything for him. But I never should have agreed to this errand—this whole 'find a wife for Isaac' thing. What was I thinking?"

It was bad enough that he had to go all the way back to Aram-naharaim. Eliezer understood that part; Aram-naharaim, or Haran, was the "old family homestead." That's where the extended family lived. There was no way that Abraham was going to want a Canaanite wife for Isaac. Eliezer had to go back to the old country to find a wife for Rebekah.

How would he know who the right woman is? It was not as if Abraham had given his trusted servant any explicit instructions or directions. It was not as if Abraham described the ideal woman that he wanted as a wife for Isaac. And so, Eliezer invented a test. He would go to a well, preparing to get water. If a woman came forward and not only offered him water, but also offered water for his camels—that would be the woman who would be the best match for Isaac.

We might have imagined that Eliezer would have said to himself: "Let's see: the woman has to like music, dancing, and living in tents." But that wasn't going to do it. This was to be a character contest. The real test would be: is this a woman who will offer to feed the camels? Is she a kind person—not only to human travelers, but to animals as well?

One of the best tests of a person's character is how that person treats those who need the most care and those who are helpless: animals.

For this reason, a midrash says, God "auditioned" Moses by seeing how well he did as a shepherd. "When Moses tended the flock of Jethro in the wilderness, a little kid escaped from him. When he found it, he said: 'I did not know that you ran away because of thirst; you must be weary.' So he placed the kid on his shoulder and walked away."

Chances are: if you care about animals, then you also care about others. That quality of caring makes for a good wife, and for a good human being as well.

Connections

> Abraham cries when he hears about Sarah's death. What does this say about the way we express our sadness and grief? About the way we react when we lose a person or an animal dear to us?

> Abraham pays an exorbitant amount of money for the burial place. What does this say about the Jewish connection to the Land of Israel? Have you ever paid more than you thought you would pay for something that you wanted?

> How does the way that someone treats animals demonstrate his or her character? Do you have a pet? How has that helped make you a better person?

> What do you think Isaac and Ishmael said to each other at Abraham's funeral? Have you ever had a tense situation with someone where you finally made up? What was it like? What did you learn from that experience?The Haftarah

THE HAFTARAH

❖ Ḥayyei Sarah: 1 Kings 1:1–31

King David was the greatest of the Israelite kings, as well as arguably the most complicated character in the entire Bible. He was a warrior, romantic figure, musician, poet—a man of deep emotions, a man who loved and lost. He was a man of great accomplishments and grave mistakes. More is remembered and written about David than anybody else in the Bible.

As in the Torah portion, which speaks of the final days of Abraham, David is now dying, and it's not pretty. The warrior-king is so feeble that he is now lying in bed, unable to get warm. Back then they didn't have electric blankets or portable heaters, so his courtiers bring him a young girl, Abishag, whose job it is to keep the old king warm. And, as feeble as he is, David is forced to confront the rebellion of one of his sons and the need to establish his true successor.

David's son Solomon was to have succeeded his father, but David's arrogant younger son Adonijah runs around and starts boasting that he will be king. He gets Joab, the commander of David's forces, and Abiathar, the priest who had been his father's lifelong friend, on his side. Adonijah throws a huge feast, but doesn't invite Nathan the prophet, nor Solomon. Nathan tells David's wife Bathsheba that her son Solomon was to have been king, and Bathsheba then tells the dying David that if Adonijah is proclaimed king, she and Solomon will be killed as traitors. David sees that this is true and ultimately Solomon is proclaimed king.

Abishag

Imagine: God summons a huge group of people together and says: "You are going to be characters in the Jewish Bible." God starts giving out parts, and a very sweet, shy, young girl raises her hand, timidly, and asks, "Do you have any *really* small parts?"

"Sure," says God. "You can be Abishag. King David will get old

and feeble. All you will need to do is get in bed with him and . . . ."
"Wait!" Abishag says. "Hold on right there!" God smiles: "Relax.
There won't be any 'funny stuff.'" "Well, okay, then," says Abishag,
still a little tentative.

So, let's wonder aloud about Abishag; this minor character who is
almost forgotten, but not quite. The question that naturally comes
to mind: did King David and Abishag not "do it" because he was too
old? No, said the ancient sages: Abishag took charge of the situation.
Abishag did not want to be alone with the king unless he married her.
As it is written in the Talmud, "Abishag said to King David, 'Let us
marry,' but he said, 'You are forbidden to me.'" Perhaps David didn't
want any more children who could then demand that they were in
line for the throne. He had had enough of that already. The sages believe that both parties acted responsibly and that Abishag was more
like a caretaker.

Poets have been attracted to Abishag's character. The Yiddish poet
Yitzhak Manger imagines Abishag missing her family and angry at
how she is being used:

Abishag sits in her room
And writes a letter home:
Greetings to the calves and sheep—
She writes, sighing deeply . . .
King David is old and pious
And she herself is, 'oh, well'—
She's the king's hot water bottle
Against the bedroom chill . . .
More than once a night
She softly mourned her fate.
True, wise people say
She's being charitable.
They even promise her
A line in the Bible.

The great American poet Robert Frost imagines her later years:

The witch that came (the withered hag)
To wash the steps with pail and rag
Was once the beauty Abishag.

Except maybe that wasn't how it really turned out. Remember, Abishag came from Shunem. Some sages said that the woman in Shunem who offered hospitality to the prophet Elisha was, in fact, Abishag. While far-fetched, this is the way of the sages saying that Abishag turned out okay and went on to live a full life.

It's all too easy to pass over minor characters in the Bible, and in life. But every person has a story; every person has feelings and needs and their own unique contribution. Even the young caretaker of an old man.

❖ Notes

CPSIA information can be obtained
at www.ICGtesting.com
Printed in the USA
LVHW08s0951050818
585984LV00004B/426/P